RUDOLF STEINER EDUCATION

TEACHING ENGLISH

Roy Wilkinson

RSCP

These notes are intended for the use of teachers, parents, and all those interested in the education of the child. They are based on the author's forty years contact with Rudolf Steiner's work and thirty years practical experience in the classroom.

TEACHING ENGLISH

Reprinted 1978, 1982, 1984, 1989, 1994, 1997

Printed in the United States of America.

Rudolf Steiner College Press
9200 Fair Oaks Blvd.
Fair Oaks, CA 95628

TEACHING ENGLISH

English, or whatever the mother tongue may be, is but a part of a much greater subject, namely, that of language. Although it is the object of this booklet to give practical indications which are of direct use in the classroom, it is important that the teacher should work out of a knowledge of the whole background. Particularly in a Rudolf Steiner school, if he is taking his business seriously, the teacher will seek to build up a substance within himself out of which he speaks. The teaching of language is a vast subject with many aspects. Equally so is the teaching of English.

Language has become so commonplace that we think very little about it, but, like so much of the world that we take for granted, a little reflection may lead us to ponder on its mysteries. Somewhere, at some time, it had its origins. It has gone through stages of development. Is has various manifestations—the spoken word and the written script. It is a means of communication and dissemination of knowledge; it is also a medium of artistic expression. What is the place of grammar? Why are there so many different languages? Why teach language anyway?

In this booklet we will attempt to deal with these more philosophical aspects first, some of which may well be suitable for study in depth in the upper school. Then there will be some practical indications of a general nature followed by specific guidance for the teaching of English in the various classes. There is a little problem of overlapping with regard to literature. References will be made to foreign literature of which particular use is made in the English lesson. However, if we think far enough, such matters as Grimm's fairy tales and the Norse legends are also part of our heritage while other works such as the Bible are universal.

In some instances the information given may appear to be aphoristic. It must be pointed out that this booklet is a guide. It does not obviate the necessity for the individual teacher to acquire knowledge for himself.

THE ORIGIN OF LANGUAGE

(Education is only one aspect of Rudolf Steiner's work. There are many others. This chapter is based on indications which he gave in other fields.)

The Gospel of St. John opens with the momentous words: "In the beginning was the word, and the word was with God, and the word was God." There is reference to the "word" here but certainly something different must be understood by it than our present meaning. What was this "word" in the beginning?

In the original Greek of the New Testament, "word" is *logos*. Logos is translated into English not only as "word" but also as "reason" and "knowledge." We have it in such words as *logic*, *geology*, *anthropology*.

In the beginning then was a reason, a cause of things, a foundation, but how do we equate these expressions with "word"? It is indeed a question which is not easy to answer but the difficulty should not deter us from making the attempt.

Turning to the Bible story of creation we read: "In the beginning God created the heaven and the earth." The Hebrew word translated as "God" is *Elohim*, and this, we understand from the experts, is a plural. If it is to be translated, therefore, it should read "Gods." These Elohim or Gods are high-ranking spiritual beings. Elsewhere in the Bible we learn of other angelic hierarchies who, as Rudolf Steiner has shown, played their part in the evolution of the earth and man. The process of creation was that from these divine beings there flowed our a sort of speech-music. this was of a spiritual nature not perceptible to the ordinary human ear. Different beings created different tones and this outflowing eventually crystallized in matter and became manifest. Some sort of analogy would be to think of a formative life force which can create sea creatures which eventually form rock.

LIFE FORCE (SPIRITUAL)

↓

SHELLS OF CALCIUM

↓

LIMESTONE OR CHALK

The life-giving outflowing sounds formed the world and man.

In the Greek myth of Orpheus we have a remnant of the formative power of speech-song and even in human speech there is a faint echo of divine activity. If we think of the medium we use in speaking, the air, we can become aware that we have an ability to create forms. An ***F*** sound will create something very different from a *B*.

The Bible also tells us that God *spoke*, and that He *breathed* into man the living soul. Thus, what emanated from the Divine is incorporated not only into the physical world but also in man. The human being is a product of the creative word.

The poet Dryden was hovering around the idea when he wrote the "Song for St. Cecilia's Day":

> From harmony, from heavenly harmony,
> This universal frame began:
> From harmony to harmony
> Through all the compass of the notes it ran,
> The diapason closing full in Man.

The human being can recognize and use speech because, like the relationship of the light to the eye, language has been built into his structure. The formation of the sounds, the tone and manner of speaking are personal matters, but the sounds themselves reflect the realities of creation.

An early example of the connection between man, word, and object is given in the story of the Garden of Eden when Adam was given the task of naming things. He was able to experience the formative power of the sounds in the objects and echoed these in his own speech; hence "that shall be their name." Sound and object form one entity.

(It is often suggested that speech develops as a result of imitation but a baby will demonstrate that it is not necessarily so. Obviously some words are imitated but equally obviously something must have been created in the first place which could be imitated. A child makes up original words to express itself. It will string a whole lot of sounds together merely for the pleasure or experience of formulating them. It is evident that there is some built-in capacity in the human being for forming words.)

Before incarnating into the physical world man existed in a spiritual form. The taking-on of a bodily form was a gradual process and the possibility of physical speech developed along with it. Out of the forces of the hardening body man began to from consonants as an expression of his experiences connected with the outer world. Although music and speech separated in human experience, a musical element remains in speech and this is represented by the vowels through which man expresses his inner feelings.

Originally a word was a manifestation or expression of the inner nature of the object. Thus, in speaking, man was intimately connected with the world around. In the course of evolution he has developed into a being with a self-conscious ego, and, as such, he stands outside nature and divorced from it. When words are spoken therefore, he no longer experiences the being of things in them but accepts them as labels. When listening he does not hear the sounds except in passing, but his mind jumps straight to the meaning. Language has become a means of communication. In poetry, perhaps, where the sound is of greater importance than the content, an echo of spiritual essence remains.

Further descent into physical existence is also the reason for the development of different languages. The "sound" element is the international tongue but we have lost the faculty of interpreting it. The stories of the Tower of Babel and the Confusion of Tongues point to a stage in world evolution where both earth and the soul of man hardened. A word in one language is now translated into a word in another but the idea expressed may be entirely different. The English *tree*, German *baum*, French *arbre* may all mean the same thing but through their sounds they express different aspects of the object.

THE VARIOUS ASPECTS OF LANGUAGE

Man alone has the faculty of speech. It raises him above the level of the animal. The latter makes noises according to its needs but only the human being can formulate his thoughts and express them. The wonder of it is that it can be done within the framework of such a limited number of sounds. But in speaking the human being also has the possibility of formulating his ideas in an infinite number of ways. He has the choice of words. He can speak in this style or that, interestingly or uninterestingly, euphonically or otherwise. When swayed sufficiently, his prose may become poetic or even poetry itself.

Writing is also a faculty which has an interesting historical development and throws light on human evolution. The teacher man well immerse himself a little in this matter and study the sequence from pictures to signs, scripts and letters. The mechanical act of writing means combining a limited number of letters in various ways. In English there are 26 letters of the alphabet yet the whole of the world's knowledge can be expressed therewith.

The purpose of writing, including of course the mechanical process of printing, is to communicate. The object, therefore, of writing and printing is to produce material which will be read. Scripts or books make world knowledge readily available. It is a sobering thought, interesting in its historical and social context, that only since 1440, when printing was invented, has knowledge become widely disseminated and that only during the last hundred-odd years has the ability to read been acquired by the common man. It is also not without significance that the words "read" and "riddle" are connected with one another

In recent years it has been fashionable to pay little attention to grammar. This only shows that there is a lack of understanding for the education of the human being as distinct from training him; in teaching grammar what was unconscious is brought to consciousness. It is thus concerned with ego-development. To put it in a more simple way, learning grammar awakens the child. He becomes aware of particular aspects of his language.

When we say "bring to consciousness," this is not to be equated with intellectual understanding. Thus, if we explain that everything has a name and that nouns are the names of things and that there are things which exist separate from ourselves, we demonstrate already a certain objectivity. In the verb there is activity and we do not stand opposite activity as we do with things, so that through verbs we participate. Since most of us would agree that grass is green, there is a certain unifying element in the adjective. These abstractions do not have to be explained in the younger years, only demonstrated, but they may well become an object of study in the upper school.

Grammar, like language and speech, belongs to the human organism, and the development of grammar reflects human development and constitution. Thus, if we think of the three main parts of speech, noun, verb, adjective, we have a manifestation of the three soul qualities of the human being: thinking, willing, and feeling. Syntax, cases, the use of the preposition, show us how the mind of man works. The use of figures of speech and the imaginative pictures in many of our words, which have now become concepts, show its development.

In teaching grammar therefore, we are working with forces that are within the human being and we are not imposing, as would often seem to be the case, something from outside. The all important thing is how to teach it.

With language, as with other subjects, the teacher should know why he is teaching it, not merely do it because it is in the curriculum or because it is conventional.

That it is a means of communication is recognized but in the present state of the world it appears to be used sometimes as a means of confused or non-communication. This is a moral question and has an enormous bearing on education and hence on the future of mankind. Thus it is essential to come to grips with language to discern if what is said or written is what is really meant. Untruth can also be spread unwittingly because of inadequacy of expression. There is therefore all the more reason to practice clear speaking, which demands clear thinking.

A knowledge of the national literature is of course an integral part of education. The way a man speaks reveals his personality and characteristics. It is a very individual thing yet the fact that he speaks a certain language connects him in an intimate way with a particular group of people and a particular world conception. To study the native tongue and its literature helps a person to understand himself, his development and his environment. Nevertheless, in so far as we are citizens of the world, life is incomplete without some knowledge of world literature. It is also an interesting thought that, as far as general education is concerned, more is probably learned from legend and literature than recorded facts.

As an art language has the same object as the other arts. The visible arts lead to a greater appreciation of the object by the beholder. Poetry enables the listener to better understand and appreciate the object of the poem; or the very sound of the language provides an inner satisfaction.

All these matters are of importance, but there is yet something deeper in studying language which the reader may have gathered from the preceding chapter. It is this: language is a manifestation of the Divine, and ultimately, the study of language leads to an understanding of the Divine and man's connection with it. In this sense, it is a religious study.

CHILD DEVELOPMENT

It must be borne in mind that in the Rudolf Steiner school the material and the way of presentation accord with the chronological development of the child. It is therefore necessary to give a brief outline of these matters. Fuller information can be found in the recommended literature.

In the Rudolf Steiner school there is no formal education before the time of the second dentition at the age of six. From the age of six to that of fourteen the children are taught "main lesson" subjects, of which English is one, by the class teacher. The arrangement is such that this teacher takes the class for a two hourly period every morning over the whole eight years. He deals with a particular subject for a period of weeks and children are encouraged to produce an artistic main lesson book for each subject. English as such, will probably be studied for three or four weeks every term up to the age of fourteen, with less time devoted to it as knowledge and proficiency increase. It may be necessary to have regular extra practice periods and a certain amount of drill is unavoidable. Drill, however, is not necessarily drudgery and a great deal depends on the way the instruction is given.

As with all subjects, the pedagogical aspect is the most important, not the mere imparting of knowledge. Therefore one must be asking continually: "What do I teach in order to further this particular faculty of the child?" Or the question could be: "How do I co-ordinate the subject matter and the way of presentation to accord with the child's development?" The answer to these questions is to be found in a study of the growing child.

Between the ages of six and fourteen the approach must be artistic. That is to say, the teacher must clothe his instruction in pictorial imagery. It must appeal to the imagination and the feeling life. After fourteen, when the intellectual powers have developed, matters can be approached in a more adult way.

When it is suggested that the approach must be artistic, it means that it must be lively, imaginative, appealing to the heart of the child rather than the head. But there are staging posts. At seven the child is in somewhat of a dream world; at nine he becomes more aware of the outer world as distinct from himself; at twelve he descends still further into material existence and at the same time intellectual faculties develop. At fourteen he becomes physically mature with independent powers of perception and judgement. The teaching must be scaled to meet the growing powers and further their particular development.

PRACTICAL WORK—GENERAL

So far we have mentioned matters over which the teacher may well meditate in order to improve his own understanding. We will now turn to actual teaching practice and deal first with general applications, to be followed by special indications for the different classes.

There is, of course, never any end to teaching or learning. One reaches a certain stage and progresses to the next. As far as the mother tongue is concerned it is also a continuous process since that is the medium of all other instruction. Certain matters have to be dealt with all the time; some can be given in periods but rarely is one explanation enough. What is expounded at one time needs to be re-explained again, possibly elaborated later, and continual practice is essential.

SPEAKING

It is a sine qua non that the teacher should speak clearly and correctly. In addition to clarity and accuracy, what has to be said should be formed artistically. There are dozens of different ways of saying things, and English is particularly rich in its vocabulary. It contains something like 600,000 words, so that no one should ever have difficulty in finding a word. To speak well one also needs an imaginative mind and an ability to conjure up pictures in words. These matters are, of course, part of teacher training and lesson preparation.

Looking back over my own boyhood experiences, I have horrible memories of teachers standing in front of the class with their hands in their pockets, droning away and sending us into a state of somnolescence for which we were blamed. Although not every teacher is a dramatic artist, he can at least seek to be effective by bringing speech to greater consciousness and by practising speech formation. Reciting aloud with attention to enunciation is a good exercise. Another is to practice speaking while walking, taking a step for each syllable. If the teacher can bring a little feeling and enthusiasm into his classroom discourses, who knows, far from sleeping, his charges may show interest.

Let the teacher also be conscious of the significance of sound. (If he has an opportunity of practising eurythmy, it will be beneficial.) There is an unfolding quality in the *L*, an enclosing in the *B*; *F* has an outflowing movement, *K* is hard, while *W* has a certain magic. Besides this significance, there is also a purely physical differentiation in the sounds, giving them individual characteristics, e.g. the explosive sounds of *D T B P G K* are quite different from the fricatives such as *S* and *F*, and these again have an entirely different character from the sounds which give movement, such as *R* and *L*.

There is also the purely technical matter of bringing to consciousness the position of sounds in the mouth. For instance, *F* and *V* are formed between upper teeth and lower lip; *S* and *Z* on both sets of teeth; *B* and *P* are on the lips; *G* and *K* at the back of the throat; the tongue is behind the upper teeth in *L N D T R*.

These are matters which will help the teacher in his own speaking. For the child of younger years they are not material for instruction, although they become so at a suitable age.

It has become fashionable in schools for the teacher to do little talking on the principle that children should find out for themselves. Thus a very potent force in education is deliberately neglected.

The direct communication from teacher to taught is something for which there is no substitute. In the younger years stories can be told as an artistic experience. Later, children can learn something about the world from one who has had experience, and this gives them pleasure. However, the teacher must realize, and most do, that hearing is not listening and neither are cognate with understanding. He must therefore be an artist with words, clothing whatever he has to say in a suitable garment so that the children's interest is kept. The direct telling of a story has a much greater impact than reading. In a sense the written word is a fossil. Writing and printing are a sort of shadow existence. Direct communication from spirit to spirit is absent. Telling or re-telling means that the teacher must have digested the material and must be active in producing or re-producing. His material becomes endowed with the living quality of his personality, and personal relationships are important.

Obviously in the course of time, children must also learn to read, and to read with understanding, but let the introduction and the process be gradual and let them learn to read at the right stage in their development. There is no advantage in learning to read early as is advocated by some educationalists.

As already mentioned, in speaking, or in writing for that matter, there is a moral aspect involved. In speaking it is important that children should not only enunciate and articulate correctly, but also that they should learn to formulate proper sentences and be able to express themselves clearly. It is a question of truth.

To begin with, speaking is learned by listening, so let the teacher speak well. If the children can then practice proper speaking, by giving a resume of their lessons or by some original contribution or by retelling a story, then the battle for proper writing is at least half won. One has to admit to a certain difficulty in this respect when classes are large. In another way, however, speaking can be practiced fairly easily and frequently and results will be beneficial. We refer to recitation or the speaking of poetry. Reciting poetry can be done throughout the school. It provides an excellent beginning to the day. It can be done in chorus with occasional individual efforts. Not only can the teacher help in the matter of articulation and speaking-out, but this activity regulates the breathing and thus has a health-giving effect. It also introduces a social element into the class. One should not be surprised to discover what can be accomplished en masse, the individual child finds difficult to do alone, but nevertheless he should be encouraged.

WRITING

It is annoying and insulting to receive a letter or a communication which is difficult to read on account of the poor handwriting. Undecipherable signatures are possibly the result of arrogance or ignorance. In any case it would appear to be reasonable and polite to produce a script that can be read. Legibility, and perhaps a little artistry, are therefore things to be encouraged in teaching children to write, as well as clarity of expression.

GRAMMAR

In the more distant past there has been much sinning in the teaching of grammar. It has been presented in such a dull schematic manner that it has appeared to have little relevance to anything in particular. Is is even thinkable that dull teaching affects the life processes of the child and so adversely affects its health. Present antipathy to the teaching of grammar may be the result of the way it has previously been taught. It is not necessarily a dislike of the thing in itself. The pendulum has now swung so far in some cases that grammar is wholly neglected or considered unimportant.

But grammar, like everything else in the world, has its place. To teach it , however, it is essential to have some knowledge of what it is a and why it should be taught, in addition to the technicalities. It is not dull if a proper approach is made.

In the first place the teacher must study grammar and be interested in it. Maybe children will find that learning about some particular aspect is not especially interesting, but they will also learn for love of their teacher if the relationship is a proper one, and they will certainly be inspired by his enthusiasm, or otherwise.

In the actual teaching of grammar, which starts at the age of nine, the approach should be made from the artistic angle. Let the teacher formulate a sentence or he can be given one by a pupil. Then he will point out that there is a doing part, a naming part, and possibly something descriptive. This will lead to an explanation of the parts of speech and eventually to the terminology. The Latin words will not mean anything at first to the children and these expressions should be explained together with the significance and use of the part of speech itself.

A similar approach can be made in the matter of syntax although the child is not ready for this before the age of twelve.

Let the teacher speak a sentence in a plain, matter-of-fact, neutral tone. Then let him repeat the statement as a question. Naturally there will be a difference in the line of delivery which the class will notice. Let him then speak a sentence with a subordinate clause, speaking the latter quicker or in a different tone. In this way there is a living quality in the instruction.

Punctuation is also something which can be taught in the first place from speaking without any knowledge of the symbols. The sentence can be experienced musically. Punctuation can also be acted. The child can also form a sentence and then certain points are brought to its notice without necessarily using the terminology.

At some stage it should be explained what punctuation is and why it is necessary. "Punctuation" was originally known as "pointing" in early English and its object was to help the reader. (*Punctuation* referred originally to the marks made in Hebrew texts to indicate the vowels.) The words exchanged meaning about the year 1700. Since that time punctuation has related to syntax.

The names of the tenses may create a certain difficulty. Past, present, and future are quickly understood but the Latin names are confusing unless they are adequately explained. It may be argued that the use of these names is unnecessary yet it is useful to have proper means of identification.

We speak of the conjugation of a verb. What is a conjugation? The derivation from the Latin gives us the key to an understanding. *Conjugare* means "to yoke together." The conjugation of the verb really refers to all its variations. Besides the way in which a verb can express the time factor, it can also express the manner in which an action is done or described, i.e. mood. The subject can be the giver or recipient of an action, hence active and passive voice. All these matters must be adequately explained in the course of grammar teaching if the children are to make any sense of this.

In general, grammar and syntax should be studied from sentences expressly formed to illustrate the rule. The rules should be derived from the examples and memorized. the children can then make up their own examples. The mistake is often made of teaching a thing once and then assuming it is understood. Continual practice and effort are essential. By Class Eight everything in the way of grammar should have been covered and generally understood. Some time can be devoted to revision in class Nine. More detailed information will be given under the respective class headings.

COMPOSITIONS

Since the pattern of work in Rudolf Steiner schools follows the chronological age, the principle also applies to the writing of compositions. A young child cannot grasp abstract ideas, neither can he formulate his thoughts logically. Proper compositions should therefore not be expected of him before the age of twelve.

The writing in the first classes can be a free reproduction of stories which have been told. Here the theme itself provides the guiding line. Otherwise compositions should center on descriptions, observations, or experiences taken from real life. As with speaking, there is a very important moral-social aspect to be considered here, namely, expressing the truth. In order to give a correct description there must be correct observation. It is also a moral-social matter to be able to say unmistakably what one means. There are therefore things to be practiced. Of particular value in this respect, as the children get older, are all matters appertaining to business, as for instance, making reports, giving information.

Up to the age of ten there should be no compositions as such. Then a start can be made with proper instruction and by the age of fourteen, pupils should be fairly accomplished. The sequence of work in accordance with the development of the child is as follows:

CLASS	CHILD'S STATE OF MIND	WRITTEN WORK
1/2	Dreamy	Retelling and relating
3	Interested in the world, with growing feeling of selfhood	Descriptions from practical life and nature
4/5	Conscious of time element, More aware of relationships with others	Private and business correspondence
6	Greater awareness of physical world and own independence	Objective reports, exact and factual descriptions
7/8	confused by problems of puberty	Original compositions, assessments

At all stages themes can be chosen from the regular school work.

What is here suggested as written work for a particular age accords with the child's development at that age. It is not to be understood as being exclusive and obviously what has been once learned should be continually practiced.

For the teacher of a large class there is always the problem of marking. Mistakes must be pointed out but to do this for everyone on an individual basis is extremely time-consuming. If a certain theme has been set, the teacher might pick out the most common mistakes and give general guidance. Until proficiency has been reached, it is better for the teacher to correct one thing only at a time, i.e. in one set of compositions , the spelling; in another, the punctuation; in the third, the grammar, etc. Obviously children must go over their own work and produce correct versions. This is discipline for the pupils and discipline for the teacher who must see that it is done, and done properly.

LITERATURE

From a purely pedagogical aspect certain stories or certain studies are particularly useful at certain ages and such material might be used throughout the whole year, not only in the English periods. It is given by the teacher as an artistic contribution to the lesson, informative in later classes. Since, however, these matters come under the general heading of English, it is right that they should be mentioned here.

As the child grows, its consciousness is changing from a dreamy, out-of-this-world state to one of wakefulness in the physical world. A series of stories which reflect this development accompany the child. They range from fairy stories in the early years to factual historical matters later.

For the child's own reading a similar pattern is to be recommended. Some indications as to suitable literature will be given under class headings.

Reference was made to poetry and drama in the chapter on speaking. Throughout the whole of their school life children should become familiar with poetry and plays but as subjects for study they only appear in the upper school. We shall refer to this in the appropriate place. There is no harm done if young children hear good poetry without understanding it, since they will gain an appreciation for language.

CLASS WORK
Class One • Age Six/Seven

ORAL:

We have already called attention to the importance of speaking, and at the beginning of class one, the main emphasis should be on speech and speaking. If we recall that the human race has been using speech since time immemorial and that writing and reading are comparatively recent innovations, we have the right perspective.

Speech, both of teacher and of children, is of prime importance. The teacher should speak clearly, distinctly and logically, tell stories at this age without any special dramatic effects, recite poems, describe events and everyday happenings. The children learn poems from listening and repeating. They recite individually and collectively.

As stories which have been told by the teacher are retold by the children, or as they make their own observations, corrections of grammar, sentence construction and pronunciation can be made in an unobtrusive, way. It should be done kindly without making the children feel embarrassed or hurt, and a little humour will add a great deal of spice to the dish. Fortunately, the children themselves will often provide it:

> *The piano should have castanets under it.*
> *Mr. Bierman is the man what brings the beer.*
> *If you sit on a pin, you suddenly jump up and that is*
> *an interjection.*

Plays can be acted, mainly with chorus work. Miming of plays and stories can be attempted.

It must be emphasized that the teacher should tell stories and not read them. A new teacher may feel a little apprehensive lest he dry up half way through or he may have nerves about standing in front of a class "naked" as it were. With a little practice and a little experience these difficulties are soon overcome. In addition to stories the the teacher can relate his own experiences and observations.

The telling of a story at this age should be an event in itself. There should be no attempt to point a moral or give explanations or comments in any way. It should stand by itself as a work of art and, as such, be allowed to take its own effect. The right materials for Class One are the well-known fairy stories, particularly those of the brothers Grimm.

As a medium for presenting something artistic, poetry lends itself even better than stories. It has a more artistic form and can touch deeper chords of the human soul.

Since the awakening of feelings of joy, wonder, reverence and awe are also a part of the education of the young child, poetry may well be used in this connection. We can call attention to the sun which never tires of bestowing light, warmth and life, and then learn, for instance, some verses from Blake's poem, "The Echoing Green":

> The sun doth arise
> And make happy the skies, . . .

This might be followed by his poem on "Night":

> The sun descending in the west
> The evening star does shine, . . .

If the teacher is speaking about water, he might use Tennyson's "The Brook." But English literature is full of nature poems which can be used in general teaching as a stimulus to the imagination and to the feelings.

There should be no explanation of poems. It can be pointed out that poems have a different quality from prose; that there is rhyme, rhythm and melody. If the contents are difficult or if the construction makes it difficult to follow, mention of the general theme can be made in advance but otherwise the poem should be inviolable.

WRITING:

One of the first things the child begins to learn on coming to school is to write. It is a subject to which, as grown-ups, we give very little thought. We accept the fact that people can write and read, almost as we expect them to speak. Indeed, for some of us, the art of writing was acquired at such an early age that we remember nothing about learning it. The gift has been with us from the beginning in the same way as speaking and we no longer make especial note of these curious symbols which form themselves into words. Our minds jump immediately to the content.

However, writing is something foreign to the small child, since, for the most part, it is an intellectual activity to which he has little relationship. The only parts of the body actively engaged are the finger tips which hold the pen and, to a slight extent, the wrist. Moreover the letters themselves have become abstractions.

Rudolf Steiner continually emphasizes the fact that for the first seven years of its life the child is pre-eminently occupied with the formation of its physical body. This reaches a certain stage of completion when the second teeth develop and forces become free to cope with other tasks. Up to this time then, the child should not be engaged intellectually. Real lessons can begin at about the age of seven and suitable ways of presenting the letters of the alphabet to the child must be found so that it is not overburdened. What are these signs which we call letters and make into words in order to communicate with one another? The Red Indians were convinced that the Palefaces communicated with each other by means of little devils. They felt that there was something uncanny in these signs which we use and no doubt they were right. They are not real. There is, however, a reality at the basis of the sign, namely, a picture which in the course of time has got lost. The modern letters of our alphabet are the end of a long process which began as pictures.

Usually we think of one alphabet but actually the children have to learn four. There are capital and small letters for writing and the same for print. The adult mind does not often realize the difference between the capital and the small letter, the written and the printed.

We must bear in mind that the child has no use for abstractions and intellectualism. He lives in movement with his body and in pictures with his mind. To present the letters pictorially therefore is correct from the child's point of view and conforms with the historical basis of writing. But there is one further important thing to be borne in mind and that is that the letter of the alphabet expresses a sound made by the mouth. The sound itself expresses something else (see the author's booklet on *The Development of Language*), and this something which becomes speech manifests a human experience.

A certain sound expresses a definite characteristic. The sound represented by the letter *B* expresses "enclosure." *L* is an unfolding. In the art of movement known as eurythmy these qualities of sound are expressed in gesture. It is therefore a great help to make use of eurythmy to bring to the children an understanding for the sounds which the letters represent.

In teaching children to write these various matters should be brought into relationship with one another.

One of the first things that should be brought to the consciousness of children in a new class is the fact that they have hands and feet. With the hands they can make and do things; with the feet they can stand or walk,

Children at this age are still living very much in activity and as a preliminary to writing, this activity should be harnessed. They can walk in different directions, follow a straight or curved line. From this it is only a step to walking or running simple forms like a circle or a loop. There is no difficulty in getting them to do this, sometimes singly, sometimes altogether: lines, circles, loops, double and inverted loops, waves, all sorts of variations and combinations. It can even be made into a fine game of Follow My Leader. At first it may be necessary to chalk the forms on the floor but this can quickly be dispensed with. In such activity some feeling for form can be developed in the whole body. The forms are then drawn boldly on fairly large sheets of paper or on the blackboard. In time, the forms become letters, although they may not immediately be recognized as such.

D Y L are loops, lines, and curves in a definite sequence.

In the outer sense, the letters of the alphabet consist of lines, but the child should be led to the actual form of the letter through a picture. Obviously all the letters cannot be taught by this means. For one thing, it is extremely difficult to find pictures in all instances, and for another, there must be time left for other subjects in the curriculum. Sufficient pictorial teaching can however be given to illustrate that a reality forms the basis of the letter. It may be objected that the teacher does not and cannot know the original picture. For our purpose it does not matter. The object is to convey the underlying truth, not any particular detail, and so the teacher makes his own pictures. He has to develop his own creative faculty and also decide where he will begin. The cursive capitals, with their loops and curves are more artistic and dynamic than their prosaic printed brothers and would therefore seem to be first choice. First of all the children should be shown a complete sentence. Then their attention is drawn to the fact that it contains separate words; then that the words are made up of letters. The teacher must then add that he is about to explain the mystery of writing and how the letters came into existence.

Next comes a painting sequence. The children can paint many pictures using simple water colour washes and while they learn something about the technique of painting and the use of colour, they are led towards writing. They paint, perhaps, blue mountains and yellow sunshine; green fields and a red sunset. Sometimes the colors have free play and form themselves into dragons, giants, or anything else which appeals to the fantasy of the particular child. If we look at a landscape, the hills and the sky are the real things. Where they meet a line is formed, but the line is not real. When we paint a landscape, we paint the hills and the sky and an apparent line appears where the two colors meet. This is the way to introduce the child to the line. Thus we paint pictures of mountains, valley, waves, boats, and so on. The children have a wonderful time with the flowing colors and are immensely absorbed in their activity.

Having achieved something approaching the desired form, the teacher can tell a story about a traveller in the days before man had learned to write, who wished to communicate with his friends. He wanted to tell them of his journeyings over mountains, through valleys, across the seas in a boat, etc. At first he drew pictures and sent them, but he found that this took a long time. Instead therefore of drawing the mountains and the sky, he made a line where the two met.

With use, and as other people copied the idea, the shapes were changed a little and we finally got *M* with which Mountain is written; *W* for Waves; *V* for Valley and *B* for Boat.

Thus one can develop most of the letters from a picture. The nest point to be dealt with is why the symbol for *B*, for instance, is pronounced the way it is. We have *B* for Boat, but what is the experience contained in the sound *B* ? We said already that in the sound *B* there is some idea of enclosure. In eurythmy, where the sound is translated into movement, this idea becomes visible gesture. The *B* movement is a reaching forward with the arms as if to enclose something which is then held firmly, almost like an affectionate embrace! (fig. 1)

Fig. 1

If we look at this gesture sideways, it is not difficult to evolve the shape of the *B*. In this case, therefore, we have been able to develop the written character *B* from the picture of a Boat and also from a bodily gesture which expresses the meaning of the sound. We have connected the written symbol *B* with the sound *B* and with human experience. This process is not possible with all the letters, but a sufficient number can be treated to give the child a sense of these relationships. It does not mean, of course, that he grasps all these things intellectually.

To help develop a feeling for the sounds and to practice the gestures, the following verse can be used in the eurythmy lesson, or merely, for recitation:

Let us bravely now build with fine bricks
Both a high and handsome new house.
That it first may be firm and well founded,
We will dig a good depth for foundations.
On the clay we will cast moulds of concrete,
Then we'll make and we'll mix a good mortar
And bricks layer upon layer we will lay
Till the top is as tall as the trees.
As it grows we leave gaps for some glass
That the sunlight in splendour may stream in.
It has views o'er the vale and the valley—
With its polish and paint it looks proud
And we know we have nothing neglected.

So far only consonants have been discussed. Teaching the symbols for the vowels is another matter entirely, not only on account of their different nature but also because of the absolute lack of logic in their combinations and pronunciation.

Consonants were originally the imitation of something in the outer world. Vowels are an expression of man's inner nature. They express something of his reaction to the outer world. We therefore have to approach them a little differently. With a knowledge of eurythmy the written character, as well as a feeling for the nature of the sound, can be developed from the gesture.

A further difficulty lies in the absence of a standard pronunciation:

Old Meg she was a gipsy
And lived upon the moors.

Should "moors" rhyme with "doors" or is the oo sound in moors to be pronounced like the oo in moo; and how can we explain rough, though, through, cough, bough?

One has to adopt some sort of standard and perhaps the easiest approach is to take the pure vowel sounds in sequence and explain alterations and variations later as a process of development. This sequence is according to the way the sounds are formed from the back of the mouth to the lips:

A (farther)
E (they)
I (feet)
O (roll)
U (spoon)

In English we have the E (ay) sound in its purity only in the short version as "fed," although in some parts of the country, Leicestershire for example, it is to be found. Possibly this is a re-distortion, but the phrase "He said to me" could sound something like this, "Ay said to may." Similarly we have only the pure I (ee) short as in "bill," while the U (oo) is a law unto itself.

To help acquire a feeling for the significance of vowels a little verse can be practiced (in eurythmy where possible) which makes use of characteristic sounds. Suppose we are standing on top of a high mountain. Around us are other peaks, some covered with snow. In the valleys are wisps of mist. It is early morning, a little cold; the sun has not yet risen. We look towards the east. The sky begins to redden; the stars grow faint and slowly from behind the mountain the sun rises. We greet the sun with the opening out eurythmy gesture of Ah (fig. 2) saying: "Ah, father sun, a marvel thou art to banish darkness and gladden the heart." From this gesture it is not so difficult to develop Λ and A, A.

Fig. 2

In a similar way the symbols E (ay), I (ee), O, U (oo) can be developed from the gesture and each time we have a saying containing these sounds. The meaning of each saying is characteristic of the significance of the most prominent vowel sound. In E (ay) something of the feeling is expressed, "The world has done something to me, I must protect myself." The gesture is a crossing of the arms. I (ee) contains something of self-assertion, O a loving unfolding, U (oo) is the opposite of Ah, being squeezed or pressed—a feeling of fear.

These written characters can be developed out of the eurythmy gesture. Obviously those not familiar with the art must find another way.

The story continues that, as we watch, the sun rises and blinds our eyes (E mood), we can feel warmed and invigorated (I mood). We want to gather the sun's warmth to ourselves (O) but we also rememeber that night, cold and dark, follow the day (U). The whole verse is as follows:

Ah, father sun, a marvel thou art, to banish darkness and
    gladden the heart.
Dazed by thy rays, our eyes we wend away, yet unafraid we stay.
We see thee in the east. We reach to greet thee.
    Our strength increases.
O, in our own souls we would enfold thy gifts of gold.
Thou movest through the blue. The earth soon cools.
    The moon then rules.

From the learning of the cursive capital letters one then proceeds to show the small ones. The teacher may now exercise his fantasy in demonstrating the metamorphoses. The children can now copy out a written sentence; their attention is drawn to the single words and they can now puzzle out the constituent parts of a word. For reading purposes they can then be shown the printed letters as modified forms of the script.

By the end of Class One children should be able to express simple thoughts in writing and give a simple written description. This can be from what they have heard or experienced or it can be original.

There should as yet be no routine spelling practice but a natural interest should not be discouraged.

READING:

It is a mistake to try to learn to read before learning to write. The will activity necessitated in writing should come first, the eye/head activity follows. This accords with the natural development of the child. If the process of teaching the letters has been followed as indicated, there should be no difficulty in learning to read as far as normal children are concerned.

The children learn to write the cursive script. They are then shown the variations which form the printed letters. They can copy these and practice them, possibly in some sort of color medium, and they will thus familiarize themselves with them. It is then but a step to reading and the various systems of recognition which are advocated are unnecessary.

The phonetic approach will bring the necessary results, i.e., learning the word from the sequence of sounds which the letters represent. Admittedly there are complications in English with our unsystematic use of vowels particularly and some of our curious ways of spelling; but basically the phonetic way is sufficient and everything which does not fit can be learned as an exception.

In the course of time some sort of explanation of deviations should be offered, e.g., the fact that English has developed from other languages and that the manner of speaking is different in different regions as evidenced in dialects. The silent gh in night, etc. can be explained as follows: these sounds were once spoken as they still are in a related language like German—*Na<u>ch</u>t*. In English, however, they have been retired. They are like the grandparents who were very active at one time but now take things easier and look on from a corner. But although they are not so active, they must not be overlooked. Thus it is when we use a word like "night." We only speak the sound, but when we write we must remember all the letters.

It is a help with reading if children are made aware of the fact that the letters of the alphabet have names and various pronunciations; the name and the pronunciation do not always agree.

At this age there are no actual reading lessons or periods but children can read what they themselves have written and peruse "suitable" books. (See note on recommended reading.)

GRAMMAR:
In Class One there is no formal grammar study.

LITERATURE:
At this age the child is still living in a sort of dream consciousness and should not be hurried to earth too quickly. His mind needs imaginative pictures as nourishment and the best books are those which contain text and artistic pictures, which can be animated. For example, in one of these there is a little man who can be made to chop wood by pulling a little lever. The themes of these are fairy stories, seasons, nature.

As far as learning poetry is concerned, poems should be learned from the teacher who has already committed them to memory. Short poems are best and they should be such as possess good rhymes, rhythms and music. A few have been mentioned in connection with general work but for recitation purposes a special selection should be made. Eminently suitable are the choruses of the elementals from the play *The Golden Key* in the booklet *Miscellany*: also the Shakespearean and such delightful creations as "The Song of the Elfin Miller" by Addingham; "Duck's Ditty" by Kenneth Grahame; "The Tadpole" by E. E. Gould and "The Fairies" by William Allingham.

Class Two • Age Seven/Eight

ORAL:
The work is very similar to that in Class One. The retelling of stories of descriptions from the child's own personal experience should be encouraged. Recitation should be continued, also acting and miming.

There is a difficulty in getting individual contributions if the class is large. It is a matter of organization and it may be necessary to limit this part of class work to four or five speakers daily. Children are sometimes restless but it is also a good exercise for them to learn to listen. As story material the teacher tells fables and legends **without** pointing the moral.

WRITING:
Small excerpts of poems can be copied, attention being paid to clear, well-formed script. The punctuation can also be copied and children can continue to express their own thoughts, recollections and experiences. The teacher can spell out words if asked.

READING:
The class can read together in chorus with the teacher, and take turns in reading short passages. It may be necessary and possible to organize ability groups.

GRAMMAR:
Children can be made aware of the full stop and the capital letters, possibly also the verb and noun, but the terminology is not necessary. There should be no definitions, but everything should be presented in a pictorial, imaginative way or in the form of a story. As an example, the text might be likened to a journey; the full stop is where the traveller sits down. The capital means a fresh start after a rest.

LITERATURE:
Fairy stories, legends, fables, descriptive animal stories; poetry as in Class One.

Class Three • Age Eight/Nine

An entirely new impulse should come into the teaching at the age of nine when the child is becoming much more conscious of the outside world and at the same time becoming more aware of himself as an individual. A new stage of consciousness is reached when the child feels that he stands opposite the world and separate from it. This is then a time when learning can really begin. In language study it is the time when grammar can be understood and from the deeper educational point of view, it is the time when grammar must be introduced so that the child's progress is furthered by bringing to his consciousness that of which he was formerly unconscious.

As attention can now be focussed more on detail, it is time to begin routine spelling practice.

The spiritual nourishment which the teacher gives is the Old Testament stories. These fit the age of the child. They show the relationship between authority and subject. It is similar to the relationship between teacher and taught. But of course they are also mighty imaginative pictures depicting human development.

ORAL:
Recitation can be practiced as usual for a few minutes daily as an opening to the main lesson and a social activity. Conversation now centers on main lesson work. Children's speech should be corrected continually. Plays. Miming.

WRITING:
An expression which has come very much into vogue in recent years is "creative writing." In our context creative writing is to be understood as that which the child produces originally. He should, however, only concern himself with what has been observed or experienced and not enter into abstract or argumentative themes.

READING:
Practice must be given in reading and this can take various forms. Reading round the class gives each individual child very little time and the faster readers get bored. Nevertheless it is possible on occasion. Sometimes the teacher can read and the pupils follow. Talents vary so that is may be necessary to form groups or to let some children read on their own while the slower ones are being helped.

GRAMMAR:
It must be remembered that, at this age, everything must be presented in a pictorial, imaginative, artistic way. Lessons must be kept alive and jolly. There is a great deal of work to be covered in Class Three but for the children it is really a voyage of discovery. They will have been using nouns, verbs, adjectives, etc. for years. Now they will discover their place and nature.

A beginning can be made with the three main parts of speech, the verb, noun, and adjective. The approach to this is to give a suitable sentence, e.g., "The cat jumps," and point out that there is a naming part and an action part. Lead on to the idea that everything we can see or think of has a name. One can refer to the story of Adam in the Garden of Eden when he was told by God to give everything a name; so too, do we give a name to everything about us.

One might even bring into the classroom objects which are quite unknown to the children and invite them to name them.

With regard to verbs it is a good idea to let the children describe all the things a stone can do, then a plant, an animal and a man. (This is also a good preparation for later studies.) Another suggestion is for one child, or the teacher, to mime or act something and the audience must guess what he is doing.

We can now explain the terminology. *Nomen* in Latin = a name, and this has become the word used in grammar for a name, the noun. Verb is from the Latin *verbum* which means the word, so we can see that the verb is very important. The verb is activity. "The cat **jumps**." The verb is the doing word. What else can the cat do? We shall soon have an abundance of verbs.

Proceeding to the adjective, we explain that it is something "thrown in or at." We may have a noun representing some object but we know little of that object unless it is described. The cat is any sort of cat, but a black cat, or a ginger cat, or a tabby cat is a special sort of cat. A cat may be black or tabby but it could also be a fat, black cat or a thin, tabby one. It could be a big, fat, black cat or an angry, big, fat, black cat. Thus one might have a game to see how many suitable epithets can be ascribed to a particular object.

Another way of introducing the parts of speech would be to refer to the period on housebuilding where it has been explained how each workman has some particular job to do. In the same way words have particular jobs.

A different approach would be for the teacher to speak a passage which consists predominantly of nouns; then one with many verbs and one with a multitude of adjectives. The children will certainly notice the different characteristics produced. This sort of thing should be brought home to them in any case.

For practice the children can write out a passage and underline the various parts of speech in suitable colors, blue for nouns, red for verbs, green for adjectives.

At a suitable moment the types of nouns should be explained and there must be adequate practice in recognizing these things.

Punctuation should in the first place be learned from listening, or it can be made into a great acting game. The teacher speaks a passage. The children stand as a sentence begins. They sit for a full stop, [period] snatch a breath for a comma, make a gesture for a question mark, open the mouth for quotation marks, jump for an exclamation mark.

Another approach to punctuation could be symbolic-pictorial. The question mark is the ear—listening in order to give the answer. Quotation marks are the lips drawn round the words actually spoken but as a whole the drawing takes too long, only indications are made. The stop is a little log such as was formerly used as a brake on a cart wheel; and the comma is the log not quite at rest.

Gender and plurals can be explained and comparisons made with foreign languages. (There are three genders in German, two in French. The ancient peoples felt the being of the object to be either masculine, feminine, or neuter. In English most objects have become neuter. A ship is still "she.") In the matter of gender it will be of interest to learn the masculine and feminine forms, e.g. dog, bitch; bull, cow; lion, lioness; lord, lady; etc.

Although it is too early at this stage to enter into the study of sentence construction, some idea of what a sentence is can be given. In most sentences there is a naming part and a doing part and sometimes, something that receives the action of the doing part.

The boy is eating.

The boy is eating an orange.

There can be an addition to the naming part by saying:

The boy who is wearing a blue coat is eating an orange.

Indications can be given that not all sentences are plain straightforward statements. They may be questions, orders, or exclamations. This is demonstrated by a suitable tone of voice.

As the child's consciousness and powers of observation grow, there can be increasing spelling practice as necessary.

LITERATURE:
Old Testament stories, legends, stories of the saints, folk tales, descriptive stories connected with main lesson work, good lyrical poetry.

Class Four • Age Nine/Ten

At this age it is both possible and necessary to introduce much more grammar and to demand much more work. The process of development in the child is one of a growing awareness of self as an entity distinct from the rest of the world, and a greater realization of time. This has its bearing on grammar but the presentation must still be imaginative.

Recommended for the story part of the main lesson are the Norse stories or scenes from ancient history.

ORAL:
A few minutes spent in choral recitation brings the class together in a common activity, regulates the breathing and generally has a harmonizing effect.

Conversation should centre round the main lesson work. This is an opportunity to recapitulate the work of the previous day. Blatant mistakes can be corrected on the spot.

It might be possible to produce a play with individual parts. This, of course, demands much more time and an English period may well have to be devoted to it.

WRITING:
What was begun in Class Three can be continued. Instruction should be given in the writing of letters. Stories are usually preferable as they provide

a theme. Other work is inclined to be chaotic. Abstract themes, expressions of opinion should be avoided as the child's mind is in no state as yet to deal with these.

Written work should be corrected in spelling and grammar in so far as these matters have been studied. At this stage there can only be selective correction, i.e., for one or two things at a time. The work should be recopied, correct spellings learned and errors explained. These corrections could well be regular homework. It must be emphasized that the teacher must see that this work is properly done.

It is not feasable to explain every correction to every individual every time but the teacher can help himself by choosing the most common mistakes and giving an extra lesson on them to the whole class.

Summaries from main lesson work can be copied from the blackboard into the main lesson books. Apart from the value of the content, this is also an opportunity to practice good handwriting.

READING:
Attention should be paid to clear enunciation and intelligent reading should be encouraged. It has to be pointed out that groups of words belong together, that pauses are essential and that full stops must not be overlooked. In other words, the listener must be able to comprehend.

GRAMMAR:
Learning about person, number and tenses now accords with the child's development.

The other parts of speech should now be taught, i.e., adverbs, pronouns, prepositions, conjunctions, interjections, the definite and indefinite articles. The learning of the parts of speech means appreciating a differentiation in function. As different people do different work and all are interdependent, so the parts of speech function in order to create a sentence.

They should not be learned parrot-like as a sort of schedule. In a sense they are a little remote and abstract and it is necessary to establish a friendly relationship with them. Their significance can be explained and one way of doing this is to consider the derivation of their names. We mentioned already nouns = *nomen* (name); verb = *verbum* (word); adjective = *adjectum* (thrown or added to). The other expressions can be explained in the same way: adverb = *adverbum* (added to the verb); pronoun = *pro nomen* (in place of the name); preposition = *prae positio* (in front of the position); conjunction = *con junctionem* (a joining together); interjection = *inter jectionem* (a throwing between); article = *articulus* (joint, limb, part). (N.B. there was no article in Latin in the sense of a part of speech.)

With the above derivations in mind and the exercise of a little imagination the teacher can bring a great deal of life into what otherwise may be a rather dull subject. It must be remembered that learning grammar is a voyage of discovery. The thing is already there.

The presentation should be kept lively. Take, for instance, a sentence where several prepositions are interchangeable:

The cat jumped **into** the chair.

Substitute towards, from, over, to, and with a little encouragement the children will discover that the work of the preposition is to show the relationship between one thing and another.

A game can be played with adverbs similar to that with adjectives, i.e., find how many adverbs can be attached to a certain verb.

The interjection will be readily understood by treading on a toe or administering some such similar shock.

Continual practice is necessary in recognizing the parts of speech. It is a good idea to let children make up their own sentences using the parts of speech consciously.

The irregular plurals of nouns will form another interesting chapter. The addition of *s* is the normal way of forming the plural in English, but there are others. Sometimes there is a change of vowel (mouse, mice), or the addition of *n* or *en* (ox, oxen). Child, children is particularly interesting. *Er* is a German plural, so is *n* or *en*. Child*ren* is a double plural. These things show the relationship with Anglo-Saxon or modern German.

As a feeling of the independent self is developing, the child will now understand what we call "person" and "number" in grammar. The first person "I" is the person speaking. "You," the second person, is the person to whom I speak. "He," "she," or "it" is the person or thing separate from I and you, about which I or you are speaking.

As a general educational matter, in the human sense, the teacher might dwell a little on the uniqueness of the "I." No one can use "I" except in reference to himself. What is it that constitutes an "I"?

We said that with the child's greater awareness of time, this is the age to learn the tenses. A good pictorial, imaginative introduction to the time factor can be given by recalling the Norse story of the three Norns, which belongs to this class in any case.

At the foot of the Tree of Life are the three weird sisters, or Norns, one of whom can see the past, another the present, and the third, the future. Thus concepts of yesterday, today, tomorrow; past, present and future can be brought home. Again it is not a question of teaching something, but of bringing something into consciousness since the children are already very familiar with past, present and future tenses.

The terminology in itself is not important but it is useful to be precise in our references.

The word tense itself means time (Latin, *tempus*). In learning English we do not often bother to learn the names of tenses systematically although we have to do it when learning foreign languages. Since studies should be coordinated, some understanding of the nomenclature is helpful.

Let us ask what actually comes to expression in the tenses. We talk about the tense of a verb. The verb expresses action or activity and an activity takes place in time. It can be happening now, will happen tomorrow, or has happened already. Thus the three distinctions of present, future and past are fairly easy to define. But what of the division of past into imperfect, perfect, pluperfect? What is the difference between "I ate," "I have eaten," "I had eaten"? The word *perfect* means "completed" and "I have eaten" (the perfect) is therefore a completed action. "I ate" (the imperfect) has not the same sense of being over and done with. In the continuous form of the imperfect "I was eating" the feeling of incompleteness is stronger. Consider also the other variations of the imperfect: "I did eat," "I used to eat." The pluperfect is more-than-complete. It relegates events to the more distant past.

While on the subject of verbs, attention should be drawn to the two types, the weak and the strong, and their relation shown to German. Some reason should be given why they carry these names.

Some further regard can also be paid to sentence construction in this class but still as yet without detailed explanation. The matter should be dealt with artistically, through speaking. By modulating his voice and varying his speed, the teacher can convey the structure of the sentence, e.g.:

"The class is studying English."

This is a straightforward sentence spoken in a straightforward way.

"The class, which is mixed, is studying English."

The subordinate clause *which is mixed* is spoken more quickly and in a different tone.

He can also illustrate it by a diagram:

"The class is studying English."

"The class, which is mixed, is studying English."

All other punctuation can be introduced and explained in this class and definite rules given. Routine spelling practice should be continued.

At some point either here or in the next class, reference should be made to the existence of the two types of sound, the vowel and the consonant. If the children have been taught properly in the past, they will now appreciate the difference in that the one represents an inner feeling and the other something of the outer world.

LITERATURE:
Norse stories, scenes from ancient history, books dealing with main lesson themes (home surroundings, animals); alliterative poetry and ballads are especially suitable for this age.

✣ ✣ ✣ ✣ ✣

Class Five • Age Ten/Eleven

ORAL:
Oral work should be continued as in Class Four. The stories given by the teacher will be from Greek mythology or medieval history.

WRITING:
Facts or information given in the main lesson can be recapitulated; stories or descriptions can be written. Practice should be given in writing business letters. A simple, orderly, development of theme should be encouraged and the teacher should demonstrate this. A transition from stories, where there is a guiding thread, to individual arrangement of ideas can now be made. The teacher must show how to develop a logical sequence.

All work should be corrected on a selective basis, explanations given, and corrected work should be recopied. If work done is on a main lesson theme, the corrected version can be put into the main lesson book where practicable. Copying should gradually be abolished.

READING:
If children are sufficiently advanced, occasional practice at reading may be enough. The use of the dictionary should be taught. Occasionally the teacher may wish to read a passage to illustrate something special, such as literary style or poetic prose.

GRAMMAR:
In this class it is probably necessary to revise a good deal of what has already been taught, with minor extensions, e.g., abstract and concrete nouns, types of adjectives and adverbs.

Further chapters would deal with the comparison of adjectives and adverbs, and with adjectival and adverbial phrases.

New work with verbs would be to study the active and passive voices. To explain the terms it can be shown how the subject can be the active agent or the recipient of the action. Attention should be drawn to the auxiliaries and to the different shades of meaning according to which is used—shall, will, may, should, would, must, ought, could, might, etc. In English we have the word "do" as a verb in its own right in the sense of "accomplish" but we also use it in a peculiar way as an auxiliary: "he did not come, " i.e., the coming was not accomplished. The verb "to be" has also a particular characteristic and has to be dealt with. Children have difficulty in recognizing this as a verb since we have consistently explained the verb as a doing word, as expressing activity. Whereas with most verbs we feel some sympathy, as if we were sharing in the action, the verb "to be" is an expression of something which exists without our participation.

As the child now realizes his own independence he will have an understanding for the difference between what is reported and what has actually been said. This is therefore the time to introduce, explain and practice, direct and indirect speech.

A few happy periods can be spent in dealing with prefixes and suffixes, antonyms, synonyms, homonyms. Some of these things present an interesting challenge to the dawning intellectual faculty but can also be taken later if the children are not ready in this class.

Also with an awakening sense for the logical, it should now be possible to explain the principle of paragraphing.

It may still necessary to practice punctuation although by now this should be pretty well perfect. Weak spellers will still need encouragement.

LITERATURE:
Indian, Persian and Egyptian myths in connection with main lesson work. Greek myths, stories from medieval history, books dealing with main lesson themes (geography, animals, plants) biographies, Irish legends. There is a wide field now for poetry. The hexameter should be studied.

Class Six • Age Eleven/Twelve

When children reach the sixth class at about the age of twelve, they are changing and developing rapidly. The stage of puberty is near if not already there and they now have a different relationship with the physical world. The reasoning faculty is beginning to develop. These facts have repercussions in the matter of what is taught and how it is taught. Although little use has been made of text books up to now, and it is a tenet of Steiner teaching that the teacher shall be all-productive and in the child's early years shall appear all-knowing; at the age of twelve the children become aware that the teacher is not ominscient. A change has gradually to be made from being the authority to guiding and cooperating. The child must now learn independence and a judicious use could be made of text books in many subjects. Reading English, whatever the subject, naturally extends the knowledge of the language. An added benefit in using a text book is to stimulate individual effort and achieve economy in teaching. At this stage the latter is extremely important owing to the fullness of the curriculum.

Oral work, writing, and reading become much more fused. Work becomes a studying together with the teacher as leader.

ORAL:

There will still be main periods which deal specifically with some aspect of English but as English in our case is the medium of instruction, the teaching is continuous. On the occasions when a text book is used in the main lesson, children can take it in turns reading a passage and giving the main thought.

Recitation should be continued and there is obvious scope for speaking when plays are being studied.

The teacher can continue to provide an artistic spot in the main lesson period by telling stories of anecdotes and these can be wide-ranging. They may be of events of recent history or descriptions of contemporary events. Controversial matters must be treated with care or possibly avoided since the child has as yet insufficient knowledge on which to base a judgement.

WRITING:

When information is given directly by the teacher, pupils can take notes and write them up in essay form. The essays are corrected by the teacher before being copied into the main lesson books. This is not popular with many teachers as a great deal of work is involved. There should be no more copying from the blackboard. If spelling is still weak, extra work should be given to be done at home.

Only with the developing intellectual faculty at this age can formal composition be expected. Even so and at least until the age of fourteen, it is best to give a theme on something real or experienced. We refer again to the social-moral element, truth. It is difficult to report and describe correctly, therefore it should be practiced.

It is advisable to talk over the contents of any proposed composition. Full instruction should be given in the first place. Whether it is in connection with main lesson subjects, correspondence, reports or any other matter, the aim should be to produce statements in good, clear, logical language, avoiding jargon and catch phrases. Subjects arising out of concrete situations are preferable as the child's mind can concentrate on them more easily than on some abstruse theme around which his mind may wander and get lost.

READING:

It may still be necessary to have occasional reading sessions to ensure that children can read intelligently and it is likely that a few slow learners will need extra attention. For the most part, however, pupils will be able to read on their own as a means of acquiring knowledge.

GRAMMAR:

Learning grammar is a continuous process and needs continual practice and revision. At the age of twelve the child is ready to learn about sentence construction, known grammatically as syntax.

It is recommended that a start be made with impersonal statements, i.e., statements where there is no subject, but only activity. An example is: "It is raining." Then we transform the sentence and give it a subject: "The rain is falling." The reason for this is that human nature follows the path from activity to observation, from verb to subject.

From here we can proceed to deal with subject, predicate, object. To coordinate with foreign languages, pupils should recognize direct and indirect object and at least consider the matter of cases, i.e. nominative, accusative, genitive, dative, even if they apparently have little relevance in English.

Again, one has to establish a relationship with the terms. What do they signify? *Praedicere* (Latin) means to declare or assert, to predicate. The subject (*subjacere* = throw or lie under) is that which underlies the influence of the predicate. The object *(objicere* = throw in front of, interpose) is the thing, so to speak, on which the predicate lands.

Nominative has to do with nomen, the name. Accusative is a Latin word via the Greek meaning the goal. Genitive has to do with generation, belonging to; while dative is the "giving case (*dare* = to give).

Further study on verbs is in place here, including their classification—transitive, intransitive, incomplete. In a scholarly class one could pursue such matters as gerund, verbal noun, participles.

In earlier classes one has given some idea of the rhythm or melody of a sentence:

Now it is time to present matters in a more intellectual form. We have to explain the simple, compound, complex sentence; subordinate clauses, types, etc.

In the work for Class Three we mentioned the four types of sentences and from this we can now lead into what is known grammatically as mood.

The boy is coming.	Statement
Is the boy coming?	Question
Boy, come.	Command
If only the boy would come!	Exclamation

A statement or a question is concerned with plain straightforward fact. We therefore speak of the indicative mood. An order or a command requires the imperative. A wish is not a concrete reality, neither is a doubt, and therefore another form of the verb, the subjunctive, is used.

(Note: the subjunctive mood in English as a special form is almost non-existent. In the above examples one could say "If only the boy were to come." The "were" is almost the only subjunctive form we have left. Those with interest in pursuing the matter should consult a standard grammar.)

There is also a fourth mood, the infinitive. This is the form "to . . . " As its name implies, it is the basic form, not limited by person, number, or time. Participles, gerunds, and verbal nouns are also considered to belong to the infinitive mood.

As the reasoning faculty develops, a new element enters the teaching. What is said now applies to the next two classes and in some respect for the rest of the time at school. Beauty up to now has been more or less appreciated instinctively. Now, however, style can be studied and a sense of the aesthetic cultivated.

In accordance with what we have already described as "sound" content, a feeling can be developed for the beauty of language. Shakespeare lets Romeo say:

> Lady, by yonder blessed moon I swear
> That tips with silver all these fruit tree tops,

Does not the repetition of the *T* induce a feeling of sweetness? This is an aesthetic appreciation of sound and of course it is to be found in all true poetry. Listen to Swinburne's rolling alliterations:

> The sea is awake and the sound of the
> song of her waking is rolled . . .

Now too it is appropriate to study the figures of speech. If the meaning of the word is explained it will often provide a clue to the understanding. *Metaphor* (Greek) means "to carry across."What is it that is carried across? It is a picture in the mind with no direct comparison. *Sarcasm* is "a gnashing of teeth"; *onomatopoeia* means "word-making."

In either speaking or writing the question arises as to how the language can be enriched. We are led to a study of words, to finding the right word. We have already introduced synonyms and antonyms in Class Five. We can now study them further and much will be discovered that is quite fascinating. We may describe something as grand, large, dignified, imposing, important, eventful, magnificent, majestic, august, exalted, stately, splendid, lofty, elevated, pompous, gorgeous, sublime, superb. Which word suits our meaning best? And what is the difference in meaning of all these words?

In speaking we may like to note how the significance of what is said changes with emphasis. Try saying "Have you seen that man?" with the emphasis first on *have*, then *you*, etc.

We have referred several times to accuracy in the use of language. There is also the element of beauty which can be found in many forms. A third attribute should be brought to the pupils' notice, namely, the power of language. What is written has an effect. What is spoken has an effect. It might be hinted that we should be careful what we say and that so much of what is said today is so absolutely trivial. We might quote William Penn: "If thou thinkest twice before thou speakest once, thou wilt speak twice the better for it." We can refer to the great works of literature or the great speeches of orators.

LITERATURE:
Stories of historical characters, works of explorers, books dealing with main lesson themes—geography, natural history, physics—poetry.

Class Seven • Age Twelve/Thirteen

All the work scheduled for Class Six should be continued. In compositions such matters as starting each sentence with a different part of speech and variation in length of sentences can be practiced. There should be no more copying from the blackboard unless for some special reason. Written work can be done in connection with the lessons in science. They provide an excellent opportunity to practice correct observation and description. Practical business correspondence should be continued.

As the capacity for expression is growing along with more conscious inner experiences, the child can be made aware of new forms of expression. Let the teacher bring to the children sentences which express wish, wonder, or surprise and then let the children make up their own.

> It is my lady, O, it is my love,
> O that she knew she were. Shakespeare

How beautiful they are, the lordly ones
Who dwell in the hills, the hollow hills
Fiona Macleod.

What dire offence from amorous causes springs,
What mighty contests rise from trivial things.
Alexander Pope

In this class, and possibly extending into the next or even Class Nine, a study of proverbs is in place. It is interesting to find those giving contrary advice:

He who hesitates is lost.
Look before you leap.

A study of conventional phrases and idiosyncracies might also be undertaken, possibly in comparison with other languages. In English we have the rather weird construction with "do." We say "How do you do?" In actual fact we seldom want to know anyway. We have the continuous forms of the verb; is coming, was going, have been waiting. Sometimes we use contradictory terms, e.g., "terribly nice." What would foreigners make of expressions such as:

It boils down to this.
Let the cat out of the bag.
To drop a brick.
To kick the bucket.

LITERATURE:
Historical novels, folk legends, descriptions of other peoples' ways of life, natural science, biographies, poetry.

Class Eight • Age Thirteen/Fourteen

A great deal of work is probably still necessary in this class in connection with the pure technique of writing. Continual practice and continual suggestions for improvement are essential. Nevertheless, if the children concerned have average intelligence and if they have been taught properly, they should now be able to write clear, coherent and near-accurate English. It should be possible to point out all mistakes in their written work and they can probably correct most of it themselves. Where necessary, exercises should be given for specific problems.

Oral work and reading should be continued. Vocabulary should be continually and consciously extended and the etymology of new words studied. Various types of sentence construction should be encouraged. Some pupils may be sufficiently advanced to work straight into their main lesson books. On occasion perhaps, subjects can be discussed and the salient points dictated.

Themes for compositions can now be given where the pupil's own capacity for perception and judgement can be brought into play. There should be further studies in style, with contrasts and some imitative writing both in prose and poetry, e.g., in the style of Dickens, Macaulay, Shakespeare.

Some main lesson periods, either here or in Class Nine, will be devoted to the study of poetry and the aesthetic appreciation of language. As far as poetry is concerned, all matters dealing with metre and verse construction should be studied. The respective qualities of the metre should be understood. For example, the rising metre expresses activity, the falling metre lends itself better to descriptive of informative works. English verse contains little hexameter or trochee. The English people are outgoing and not reflective, hence the rising rhythms of the English language.

A further study is that of epic, dramatic, and lyric poetry. There is a certain difficulty here as epics of the classical type do not exist in English literature except in translation, and these one has to use. It is true that some of the poetry of Milton, Byron, Tennyson and Arnold is of an epic nature but it is comparatively polished and cultivated.

The best examples of dramatic poetry are found in plays. If children are sufficiently mature to digest a Shakespearean drama, it can be an object of study. Probably one of the histories is preferable, *Julius Caesar, Coriolanus,* or one of the English kings. If the whole play is too difficult, then extracts can be taken. Children should also connect the development of drama with general history and learn something of the Elizabethan stage.

Lyric poetry exists in abundance .

Attention should be called in this threefold manifestation of poetry to the fact that it is a reflection of the threefold nature of man. There is a thinking element in the epic; willing in the dramatic; and feeling in the lyric.

LITERATURE:
Historical novels, geographical descriptions, natural science, peoples, biographies, poetry.

Summary

The foregoing represents a guide to the work to be done under the supervision of the class teacher from Classes One to Eight. The author's experience in Upper School teaching is limited. He has taught English in Classes Nine and Ten, with a small excursion into Class Eleven. Since what he writes is on the basis of experience, he does not presume to give detailed guidance for the top two classes, the age groups of seventeen and eighteen. Some useful information on these points, as well as others, will be found in the *Curriculum of the Waldorf School* by Eileen Hutchins.

In any case, specialists are responsible for the instruction in the Upper School and it is to be assumed that their knowledge is detailed and comprehensive. Moreover, talents and tastes vary, so do conditions and circumstances, and there exists an abundance of material.

For these reasons only a few of the more important indications are given here.

It is to be hoped that the teaching up to this point has provided the pupils with the necessary tools. It is to be feared that a great deal of revision is probably necessary as well as a great deal of routine practice. Boring though this may be to the Upper School teacher whose desire is to spread his wings as well as those of his pupils, it is essential. It will be necessary to continue to practice writing compositions of all sorts, doing comprehension exercises and making summaries. The teacher must keep checking and insisting on formal accuracy in such matters as spelling, punctuation and sentence construction.

Class Nine • Age Fourteen/Fifteen

Choral recitation should still be practiced and individuals might undertake some form of oratory. Good material for the former may be found in the Greek drama, with which the pupils should be given some acquaintance in any case, and for the latter, speeches from Shakespeare's plays are an obvious choice. Since the class will probably be producing a play, there is some oral work for all.

With regard to writing, some of this may well be done without guidance but instruction in special points is still necessary. For instance, sentence construction should be practiced consciously. Pupils should appreciate the difference in style whether a sentence begins with the subject, a clause or a phrase. It must also be pointed out how compositions are affected by the frequent use of certain parts of speech and by the use of figures of speech.

Compositions in various styles should be attempted, i.e., imaginative, expository, descriptive. Practice in business and social correspondence should be continued. There will be continual written work to be done in connection with other subjects.

To help appreciate the various styles of prose and poetry, the works of a number of authors with distinctive styles can be studied as suggested for Class Eight. It will be necessary for the teacher to seek out suitable excerpts.

Further to the matter of studying the aesthetic quality in language, English and foreign languages can be compared in respect of their sound value. Since all pupils in the English schools will have learned French and German, and some will probably have a nodding acquaintence with others, they can be asked for comparisons. (It is assumed that the teacher is well educated.) What is the relationship between vowel and consonant? From what area of the organism does the language proceed? It will be appreciated that English follows the billowing waves of the sea; German is plastic; French is like a light flowing breeze.

Another study for this class would be concerned with the techniques of poetry, the main outlines of which are as follows:

All life is based on rhythm. When language is enlivened, it becomes rhythmic. As the physical body is the instrument for the human spirit, so sound, metre, rhythm, are used to incorporate ideas.

Basic meters are the:

Iamb	u —
Anapest	uu —
Trochee	— u
Dactyl	— uu
Spondee	— —
Pyrric	uu

These are known as feet.

Lines can have various numbers of feet and they have Greek names. From two to six feet these are: dimiter, trimeter, tetrameter, pentameter, hexameter. When the ends of the lines have similar sounds, they are said to rhyme.

In actual fact poems are rarely regular throughout or they become boring and sound artificial.

Another form of rhyme is the alliteration which we met in Class Four.

Lines can be put together to make many different verse forms. These are some of them:

Blank Verse	unrhymed iambic penatmeters
Heroic Couplet	iambic pentameters rhyming in pairs
Sonnet	iambic pentameters, fourteen lines with various rhyme sequences
Octosyllabic	iambic tetrameters rhyming in couplets
Free Verse	no set rhyme or rhythm

Other types of poems should also be explained, i.e., ode, elegy, epigram. Examples should be given or found in all cases. The study is continued in Class Ten.

At this age of fourteen/fifteen, physical maturity and idealism clash. It is the Goethean experience of "two souls within my breast."In art the contradiction is worked out by sketching in black and white. The soul needs to expand and contract, to laugh and to weep, to experience comedy and tragedy, and somewhere there must be an anchor point from which such things can be viewed objectively.

Shakespeare provides the material likely to be of the greatest importance to the pupils' development. The individuality of the now-adolescent is making iteself felt. He is becoming conscious of his own personality, his own ego. The study then of other egos is important and nowhere are these better portrayed than in Shakespeare.

Shakespeare stands at that historic point in time when the human being achieves a greater consciousness of his ego and at the same time becomes more conscious of the external world. The characters of his tragedies face external events, and through meeting them and dealing with them, eventually that which is individual appears. Shakespeare does not portray his own experiences, but the characters speak through him and demonstrate their ego-hood. If time and inclination allow, the contrast can be drawn here with Goethe in his *Faust*.

Hamlet is typical of the new man. He was hindered from taking action by his feelings; he was "passion's slave," yet desired to act from reason, from his own ego-consciousness.

Class Ten • Age Fifteen/Sixteen

Routine work will be continued. Although a great deal is indicated here for Class Ten, it will of necessity have to flow over into Class Eleven and possibly Twelve. Also English and history become somewhat intertwined as do English and other subjects.

In each of the four classes of the upper school, a special period is devoted to the study of one of the arts, showing its relationship with human evolution. In Class Nine, this has been a study of the visual arts, particularly painting. In this, and extending probably into Class Eleven, the attention is on language. Following this, music and architecture are the subjects.

When the Greeks wrote poetry, they felt that some heavenly being was speaking through them—the Muse. Even now we speak of "inspiration," a "breathing in." It is as if some spiritual experience is inhaled and the mind lights up. This can be a source of creative activity and one way in which this comes to expression is poetry.

In poetry some moving experience is expressed in a special way in words. It can be an experience from either the outer or the inner world. It is too great for prosaic expression. A special sequence of sounds has to be created together possibly with rhyme, rhythm, and meter.

The medium of poetry is words, but words which lend themselves to adequate expression:

Mont Blanc is the Monarch of Mountains
from "Manfred," Byron

No stir in the air, no stir in the sea
from "The Inchape Rock," Southey

And the night spake, descending on the sea,
Ravening aloud for ruin of lives
from "Tristram and Isolde," Swinburne

Then the imaginative faculty is brought into play. A prose statement becomes winged when it is transformed into poetry. We might say:

The eagle stands on a rocky height,

but Tennyson transforms the prosaic statement to:

He clasps the crag with crooked hands,
Close to the sun in lonely lands.
Ringed with the azure world he stands.

In prose: *He dives down.*

According to Tennyson:

The wrinkled sea beneath him crawls,
He watches from his mountain walls,
And like a thunderbolt, he falls.

Consider, too, among many other examples, the poetic effect in Shelley's "Skylark":

In the golden lightning
Of the sunken sun,
O'er which clouds are brightening,
Thou dost float and run,
Like an unbodied joy whose race is just begun.

Or the combination of sounds and pictures in his "Ode to the West Wind":

O wild west wind, thou breath of autumn's being,
Thou, from whose unseen presence the leaves dead
Are driven, like ghosts from an enchanter fleeing,
Yellow, and black, and pale, and hectic red,
Pestilence stricken multitudes.

Metaphor and simile are figures of speech which add greatly to the picture content of a poem:

At once they rushed
Together, as two eagles on one prey
Come rushing down together from the clouds,
One from the east, one from the west.

—a simile from *Sorhab and Rustum* by Matthew Arnold.

The styles of poetry should be compared. The alliterations in "Beowulf" can be contrasted with the lyrics of Chaucer, and with the forms of the sonnets and the pentameters of Shakespeare.

Chaucer's verse is still regular. Later comes English rhymed verse, but the thought content of a sentence is important, and therefore the end of a sentence need not be at the end of a line. Shelley's "Ode to the West Wind" is a good example.

Blank verse is the most characteristic of English measures. There is no rhyme, no measured rhythm, no fixed caesura. It allows freedom of expression.

Free verse is a modern form of poetry. The older forms give the impression of constriction. Where there is a regular rhyme and beat, it sometimes appears to be thought-out. Whereas a regular meter can get tiring and even boring, free verse enlivens. It allows change. This is not to say that all modern free verse is wonderful. Some of it may be clever but also meaningless. It can also be characterized as a sign of the times.

What has previously been explained as the nature of sound can now be appreciated. In the introduction we mentioned the nature of sound in language, and the mechanics of its production. Speech exercises to bring the sounds and their formation to consciousness can now be practiced. If eurythmy is done in the school, it will help. Choral recitation is an excellent exercise. Get pupils to speak out extracts from:

"Lays of Ancient Rome" by Macaulay
"Ode on Christ's Nativity" by Milton
"Ode to the West Wind" by Shelly

and let the roof reverberate.

A study for the tenth class would be the history of the English language in connection with the development of the English people, e.g.: England has been a meeting place of the races, and out of the mixture of Celt, Roman, Anglo-Saxon, Viking and Norman has the English race been formed. Of these the Anglo-Saxons and French-speaking Normans have been predominant.

Similarly the English language has evolved from a mixture of Celtic, Latin, Anglo-Saxon, Scandinavian, and French—the Anglo-Saxon and Latin/French being the most important ingredients. This gives our language its abundance of words. One of its characteristics is the division into "intellectual" words and "will-element" words. The former come via the Latin, the latter through Anglo-Saxon.

It is a comparatively young language. Only with Chaucer did it become recognisable. It flowered in Shakespeare's time, and again at the time of Wordsworth, Shelley, and Keats.

But what has been its inner development?

Inflexions have disappeared. Pronounced grammatical forms have gone. Vowel sounds have become very varied with a proliferation of dipthongs. The richness of vocabulary allows many shades of meaning. The rhythm of words is not fixed but the tendency is towards monosyllabic expression. English provides a means of very direct speech. It is the practical language of the world and has indeed become the nearest to a world language.

In Class Eight, mention was made of epic, dramatic, and lyric poetry. It is now appropriate to extend the study to actual great works of literature. The *Iliad* and the *Odessy* are the famous Greek epics. The Aenead is Roman. From Finland comes the *Kalevala*. There are the ancient Indian epics of the *Mahabharata* and the *Ramayana*; from Persia the stories of Zarathustra. An ancient Persian story in modern dress is "Sohrab and Rustum" by Matthew Arnold. From northern Europe we have the Edda, and from central Europe the *Nibelungenlied*. From France comes the famous *Chanson de Roland*, and newer epics are the stories of King Arthur, Dante's *Divine Comedy*, Milton's *Paradise Lost* and *Paradise Regained*.

With regard to dramatic poetry we have already mentioned th plays of Shakespeare which have not been surpassed. Byron's *Manfred* is worth considering for its content.

The word "lyric" is derived from the Greek and it means: "to the accompaniment of the lyre." In other words, the lyric poem is of the nature of a song. It expresses the writer's own thoughts and feelings.

Epic tells stories; lyric expresses an immediate experience; dramatic shows present action.

A proper historical survey of English literature, including poetry and drama, is an obvious study for this class, to be continued in the next. This is normal study material, but it can be combined with a study of literature as a whole. As with other subjects, the image of developing man should be kept in mind. In teaching history we teach the story of man's development; in the History of Art period we do the same. The same theme manifests itself in the history of literature. A course of study might therefore be given entitled: Literature and the Evolution of Man, with the following as an outline:

The stories from ancient civilisations show that man and the gods were in direct contact and that people were led as groups. That is to say, the feeling for individuality was non-existent, but there was a family or race-consciousness. The teacher may now recall the stories from the mythologies which were told in Class Five and Six, and throw new light on them. What were stories now become objects of study.

The Ancient Indian, Persian, and Egyptian civilisations were all divinely led or divinely inspired. This is apparent from the stories. In Greek times there is a change, a step in the direction of independence. Odysseus is still dependent on divine guidance but in the course of Greek civilisation we meet Socrates who teaches the power of rational thought. At the same time we see individualities emerging as human beings, and not as inspired leaders. In Greek drama the gods still dictate.

The Old Testament shows us a people divinely led and acting out of group-consciousness. The New Testament shows us a new impulse of self-development. (Compare the Commandments with the Sermon on the Mount.)

In non-Christian European literature is the *Nibelungenlied*, which tells a story of love for gold, of revenge and fighting. In the contest between the two main races, the Huns and the Burgundians, there is a good illustration of group-consciousness. People are still influenced by the gods but they function at a different level from the characters of the *Odyssey*.

Contemporary with the *Nibelungenlied* is the King Arthur saga with the stories of the knights and their ideals. Their deeds were done on their own initiative. The knights prayed to the divine for help and guidance, but this is a far cry from being told what to do as in Greek times.

In western Europe the age of natural science and reliance on the physical senses begins with Roger Bacon (1214-1292). The Reformation, the great discoveries, and the conquest of the physical world soon follow.

In the drama of the period we no longer find the gods dictating , nor as yet are individualities portrayed. The actors are now characters: the aristocrat, the merchant, the lawyer, the rogue, the clown.

In Shakespeare we find the portrayal of individualities. *Romeo and Juliet* is concerned with a blood feud. In falling in love with one another the young lovers broke the family quarrel. They die, but because of their independent action, the feud is dissolved.

The contrast between the *Eumenides* by Aeschylus and *Macbeth* by Shakespeare can be very illustrative. In the former a murder has been committed by the command of a god and the perpetrator, Orestes, is being haunted by the Furies. Macbeth commits murder on his own initiative. He is haunted by his conscience. What was outer experience in Greek times has become an inner one in post-Christian times.

If time is short, as it usually is, then at least some study could be made of three epics, one classical, one medieval, and one modern.

- *Odysseus* by Homer—Here mythological incidents are interwoven with everyday occurrences. Inner and outer world are confused.
- *Nibelungenlied* (Song of the Nibelungs)—Inner and outer experience are still mixed, but a human element enters.
- *Idylls of the King* by Tennyson—Inner world and outer are quite separate.

With regard to English literature, this could only come into existence with an English language, and it was as late as 1200 before this became recognisable as an entity. The novels, the drama, the philosophical writings, scientific treatises, poetry, are all manifestations of the developing human mind, and a reflection of contemporary conditions. Chaucer's work points to an age of greater sense perception (observation). Other poets show other aspects: Shakespeare, individual striving; Milton in puritanical England, depth of thought; Pope, superficiality; Goldsmith, social understanding; Shelly, Byron, freedom; Wordsworth, observation of nature and contemplation; Scott, romanticism; Tennyson, ideals; later poets—that is a question for the pupils.

As explained in the history booklets, many things have to be taught symptomatically. If one tries to cover too wide a spectrum, then the effect is lost. The teacher must therefore be selective and pick out those matters by which he can achieve the most educationally. This could mean taking a few themes, but dealing with them thoroughly. In an historical context Chaucer is an obvious choice, so is Shakespeare. As a modern or near-modern representative, Tennyson might make up a trio. His descriptions are very exact. All his poems are painstaking in their workmanship. He wrote many types of poems and all sorts of ideas are expressed in his works, e.g., *Idyllls of the King* (Arthur), *The Lady of Shalott* (the world is a mirror), *Sunset and Evening Star* (quiet contemplation and no fear of the beyond), *The Higher Pantheism* (relation to the divine).

Class Eleven • Age Sixteen/Seventeen

Some formal tuition may still be necessary in matters of grammar, compositions, making summaries, etc. In any case, practice will still be required.

From an abundance of examples, artistic appreciation of language and literature should still be cultivated—the formation of sentences, the use of imagery, euphony, rhyme and rhythm.

The studies of Class Ten are continued. History and literature, and to some extent, science and philosophy, are intertwined. The stories of King Arthur which have been read in Class Eight can now be "interpreted." As youthful idealism wells up in the pupils' souls, they will no appreciate the ideal of the knight and the transformation of qualities required to achieve the Holy Grail, a mystic experience. They will also now be ready to consider stories which they have heard in the earlier classes and find a deeper content. Such an exercise is rewarding for pupils and teacher. An example from personal experience will illustrate the point.

It happened that I was teaching a group of seventeen year olds whom I had taught as a class teacher from Class One to Eight. We had been ranging over a whole lot of ideas such as birth, life, death, the creation of the world, the universe, God. One morning I came into the class and announced that I would tell them a story which I had told them in Class One, and which most of them remembered. It was Grimm's story of "Mother Holle."

We had already discussed allegories and symbolism, and now I gave them the task of finding what basic idea underlay this story. After a few minutes, one of the girls, with positive radiance in her eyes, came up with the answer: "reincarnation."

A further study would be of the development of language, with an extended study of words and their derivations. If individual projects are undertaken, another theme might be the development of writing. Matters mentioned in the introduction can be discussed with the pupils here.

Class Twelve • Age Eighteen/Nineteen

Formal tuition and practice should still be given as necessary. As with so many other school subjects, the object in Class Twelve should be revision and rounding-off. If the survey of English literature has not been completed, now is the time to do it and to bring it right up to modern times. Since the teacher, however, will seldom achieve as much as he would like, he must decide what is of most importance.

Apart from technical matters, the teacher should now try to give a survey of world literature. The adolescent mind is rapidly opening out to the world, and its needs should be met. The teacher should bear in mind the basic requirement of education: human development. In a certain respect he is no longer instructing his pupils but pointing out sources of inspiration so that each individual may find his own truth.

BOOKS BY ROY WILKINSON

Questions and Answers on Rudolf Steiner Education
A very popular introductory booklet.

The Temperaments in Education
A practical guide to the recognition of the four temperaments and to ways of using them educationally.

The Interpretation of Fairy Tales
The hidden wisdom in thirty-nine popular Fairy Tales.

The Curriculum of the Rudolf Steiner School

Commonsense Schooling
A concise, straightforward account of Rudolf Steiner Education.

Rudolf Steiner Education Series:

Teaching English
Teaching Mathematics
Teaching Physics and Chemistry
Teaching Geography
Teaching History I : *Ancient Civilizations, Greece, Rome.*
Teaching History II: *Middle Ages, Renaissance to Second World War.*
Old Testament Stories
Commentary on the Old Testament Stories
The Norse Stories and Their Significance
Teaching Practical Activities
Man and Animal
Plant Study–Geology
Nutrition, Health, and Anthropology
Miscellany: *A Collection of Poems and Plays.*
Plays for Puppets

Ordering information:

*Other Books by Roy Wilkinson

The Origin and Development of Language

The Spiritual Basis of Rudolf Steiner Education
The Waldorf School Approach.

Rudolf Steiner: Aspects of his spiritual world view
Anthroposophy vol. I
Anthroposophy vol. II
Anthroposophy vol. III

<u>Basic Anthroposophy Series:</u>
Twelve booklets dealing in outline with aspects of life from the spiritual scientific point of view as presented by Rudolf Steiner — World Evolution, Destiny, Karma, Inner Life, etc.

* Also available from Rudolf Steiner College Bookstore